You did not find this book by accident.

There is something within you that knows it is time.

Time to question the stories that no longer serve you.

Time to unravel what was never truly yours.

Time to step into the life that has always been waiting for you.

This journey is not about fixing yourself—you were never broken.

It is about remembering who you are beneath the layers of conditioning, expectations, and survival patterns that have shaped you.

Take a deep breath. Let yourself be here. There is no rush, no right way to do this. There is only your pace, your truth, and your unfolding.

– Belinda

Cover Design and photograph by: Belinda Evans
Edited by: Belinda McCormack
Self-published by: Emjay Spa & Wellness
Printed in Australia

For permissions, inquiries, or additional resources, visit
www.emjayspa.com

Dedication

To those who have spent their lives seeking something more.

You were never lost—you were simply waiting to be found.

This book is for you.

Acknowledgments

Writing this book has been one of the most profound journeys of my life, and it would not have been possible without the unwavering support of those who have walked with me and beside me.

To my family, for teaching me lessons in both love and inner strength. To my friends, for holding space for me even when I didn't have the words to express what I needed. I am incredibly grateful to you all.

To my clients, whose bravery and vulnerability have inspired every page of this book. Thank you for trusting me to support you in your journey.

And to my readers, who are embarking on their own journey of self-discovery—you are seen, you are worthy, and you are enough.

A special thank you to Nan, who believed in me and and my abilities long before I did, your encouragement, love and support made all the difference. Fly very high and rest in eternal peace.

Boo 🖤

This book is for those who:

- Feel like they have spent their lives **being who others need them to be** but don't know who they truly are.
- Struggle with **self-doubt, people-pleasing, emotional suppression, or feeling "not enough."**
- Are tired of **repeating the same patterns in relationships, work, and personal growth.**
- Want to **heal from generational wounds and break cycles that no longer serve them.**
- Are ready to **step into their truth, even if it feels uncomfortable or unfamiliar.**

This book is not about giving you a new identity—it's about helping you remember (or uncover) who you were always meant to be.

Introduction

What if everything you thought you had to be was never really yours to carry?

What if you could let go of the masks, the stories, and the expectations that have shaped your life—and finally come home to yourself?

This book is not just about healing; it's about **becoming real**. It is about peeling back the layers of conditioning, survival responses, and limiting beliefs so that you can step into the fullest, most authentic version of yourself.

Table Of Contents

Unwritten – Releasing the Past, Reclaiming Yourself   1

Chapter 1: Lifting the Veil – Recognising the Masks You Wear   14

Chapter 2: The Stories That Keep Us Stuck   21

Chapter 3: Rewiring & Reconnecting with Your True Self   28

Chapter 4: Integration – Living Authentically & Building Emotional Strength   37

Chapter 5: Emotional Resourcing – Creating an Inner Foundation of Safety   45

Chapter 6: Processing Anger & Reclaiming Emotional Power   53

Chapter 7: Breaking the Cycle of Self-Abandonment   62

Chapter 8: Healing Trauma Responses & Reclaiming Nervous System Safety   71

Chapter 9: Navigating Setbacks & Relapse – How to Handle Difficult Moments   79

Chapter 10: Healing the Mother & Father Wounds – Releasing Generational Trauma   86

Chapter 11: Reconnecting with Joy, Play & Inner Freedom   97

Chapter 12: The Future Self – Embodying Your Highest Potential   104

Chapter 13: Integrating the Journey & Moving Forward   110

Final Word from Belinda   118

How to Use This Book

Each chapter builds upon the last, guiding you through a process of **self-inquiry, nervous system healing, emotional integration, and self-empowerment**. At the end of each chapter, you'll find:

- **Journal prompts** to help you explore your own experiences.
- **Somatic practices** to regulate your nervous system and release stored trauma.
- **Reflection exercises** to integrate what you've learned into daily life.

Healing is not about information—it's about **embodiment**. Take your time with this book. Let the words settle into your body, not just your mind. And remember, **there is no rush to arrive anywhere—you are already enough, exactly as you are.**

Chapter 1: Lifting the Veil – Recognising the Masks You Wear

"The journey to authenticity begins with peeling back the layers." – Unknown

The Hidden Cost of Wearing a Mask

From the moment we take our first breath, we begin learning who we "need" to be to feel safe, loved, and accepted.

We learn to adapt, suppress, or perform in response to our surroundings. Some of us become high achievers, always pushing harder, believing our worth is tied to success.

Others take on the role of caretaker, putting everyone else first while neglecting our own needs. Some learn to blend in and stay quiet, afraid that speaking up will bring rejection or conflict.

These masks—the roles and identities we unconsciously adopt—helped us survive. But over time, they become heavy, exhausting, and limiting. They prevent us from truly seeing ourselves and being seen by others.

This chapter is about unmasking. It's about recognising the roles we play and understanding why we wear them. Only then can we start to reconnect with our authentic selves.

This is your invitation to explore:

- What masks am I wearing?
- How have they protected me?
- What might be possible if I no longer needed them?

Defining Key Terms: Masks, Roles & Illusions

Before we dive in, let's get clear on what **masks, roles, and illusions are**:

- **Masks** – The **personas we adopt** to navigate the world, protect ourselves, or gain acceptance (e.g., The Overachiever, The Caretaker, The Fixer, The Entertainer).
- **Roles** – The **expected identities** we take on based on relationships, work, and culture (e.g., Partner, Parent, Leader, Peacemaker).
- **Illusions** – The **belief systems and stories** we carry that shape how we see ourselves and the world (e.g., "I have to work harder to be worthy," "If I set boundaries, I'll lose people").

These **masks, roles, and illusions** form the **hidden scripts** that run our lives—until we begin questioning them.

Belinda's Personal Story: The Perfectionist Mask

"I didn't realise I was wearing a mask until it shattered."

I spent years unknowingly **living behind the mask of "The Perfectionist Professional."**

On the surface, I projected confidence—I was praised for being **exceptional at my job, efficient, hardworking, and driven**. I climbed the ranks, excelled in every role I stepped into. But **beneath that exterior**, I was drowning in **self-doubt, imposter syndrome, and anxiety. Self-sabotage followed.**

I didn't know I was **running on survival mode.**

I wasn't aware of how much **conditioning** had shaped my belief that **I had to be productive, competent, and independent at all times**—that any sign of struggle meant **weakness.** My nervous system was locked in a **constant cycle of stress and burnout.**

Every time I achieved something, I felt relief—until the next wave of pressure hit. **I was addicted to achievement, but it never made me feel truly safe.**

My Breaking Point

I didn't recognise the **warning signs** until my body forced me to. I would get **physically ill** whenever I took time off. I **ignored exhaustion, headaches, and gut issues**—rest felt like a luxury I couldn't afford. Someone close to me gently tried to help—but I **couldn't "hear"** them until I hit my **breaking point.**

Then, during a personal development retreat, **I was put on display as an example of unhealthy patterns—without warning. It felt like betrayal. As I reflect on it now, it was also the moment I woke up.**

For the first time, I saw how my **fight, flight, freeze, and fawn responses** had ruled my life:

- **Freeze** – I silenced myself to stay safe.
- **Fawn** – I became a people-pleaser, anticipating the needs of others, before my own.
- **Flight** – I used hustle and achievement to escape discomfort.
- **Fight** – I suppressed my anger until it manifested as frustration, self-sabotage, and unhealthy coping habits.

Recognising these **nervous system patterns** helped me finally **release the mask**—and start reclaiming my truth. **Everything changed when I woke up.**

The Many Forms of Masks

Here are real-life and hypothetical examples of how masks manifest. Each mask was once a survival strategy—but now, it may be keeping you from yourself.

- **The High-Achiever** – The person who always "has it together," but secretly feels unworthy unless they're succeeding.
- **The Helper** – The person who **prioritises everyone else's needs**, afraid that setting boundaries will push people away.
- **The Chameleon** – The person who **adapts to every environment** but never feels truly seen.
- **The Stoic** – The person who never shows emotion because vulnerability feels unsafe.

18

Practical Exercises: Beginning the Unmasking Process

Exercise 1: Identifying Your Masks

Journal Prompt: *What are the roles I play in different areas of my life? How do they serve me?*

Exercise 2: Nervous System Awareness

Body Scan: Close your eyes. Think about showing up **without your usual masks**. Notice where you feel **tension, discomfort, or resistance** in your body.

Exercise 3: Releasing the Old Narrative

Affirmation (If it feels safe for you):
"I am more than the roles I play. I am allowed to be seen, just as I am."

You Are Safe to Be Seen

Your masks helped you survive. But now, you are allowed to **choose something different**.

- **You are worthy** without overworking.
- **You are loved** without people-pleasing.
- **You are enough**, exactly as you are.

This is the beginning of a new chapter—one where your true self gets to breathe.

As you move into the next chapter, remember
—unmasking is not about erasing who you are.
It is about letting go of what was
never truly yours.

This process may bring up discomfort,
uncertainty, or even resistance,
and that's okay.

You are not doing it wrong—
you are simply stepping into the unfamiliar.

Take a deep breath.
Let this be a moment of reassurance.

You are safe to explore, safe to question, and
safe to move forward at your own pace.

Healing isn't about force; it's about allowing.
There is no rush.

You are exactly where you need to be.

– Belinda

Chapter 2: The Stories That Keep Us Stuck

"The body keeps the score of our experiences, even when our mind tries to forget." – Bessel van der Kolk

Understanding the Power of Our Stories

Our sense of self is shaped by the **stories we tell ourselves**—stories that often originate in childhood and are reinforced over time. These narratives aren't just abstract thoughts; they **live in our bodies, influence our decisions, and determine how safe or unsafe we feel in the world.**

For those who have experienced **trauma—whether through significant events or small, repeated moments of dismissal, rejection, or fear**—these stories become the framework through which we see ourselves and our place in the world. The mind adapts, the body reacts, and patterns are created that keep us feeling **stuck, small, or disconnected.**

But here's the truth: These stories were learned. Which means they can be **unlearned**. In this chapter, we will explore:

- **Where these narratives come from** and why they feel so real.
- **How trauma rewires our brain and nervous system**, making certain beliefs feel impossible to change.
- **Why affirmations often don't work for trauma survivors**, and what to do instead.
- **How to recognise and rewrite the subconscious stories that hold you back.**

By the end of this chapter, you'll begin **disrupting old narratives and making space for a new, more authentic version of yourself to emerge.**

The Origins of Our Stories: How Trauma Shapes Our Reality

Many people assume trauma only refers to **catastrophic events**—abuse, violence, or life-threatening situations. But trauma is **not just about what happened; it's about how our nervous system processed the experience.**

For some, trauma comes in the form of **small, repeated moments:**

- Being told *"stop being so sensitive"* as a child, making you believe your emotions are too much.
- Learning that **love and approval must be earned** through achievement, leading to a relentless drive to succeed.
- Feeling dismissed or ignored when expressing pain, making self-silencing a habit.
- Witnessing **unpredictable or emotionally unsafe environments**, leaving your nervous system in a constant state of alertness.

The brain and body **internalise these moments**, shaping our core beliefs and survival responses. Over time, these patterns become **automatic**—until we consciously work to change them.

The Science: How Trauma Programs Our Beliefs

The Brain & Survival Mode

The brain's primary role is **not happiness—it's survival.**
When we experience something that makes us feel
unsafe (physically or emotionally), the brain:

1. **Records the experience** as a warning for the future.
2. **Creates a belief** to help us avoid similar pain (e.g., *"I must be perfect to be loved"*).
3. **Stores the response in the nervous system**, so we automatically react without thinking.

This is why **affirmations don't work for trauma survivors**—saying *"I am worthy"* means nothing if your nervous system **is wired for survival and still believes the world is unsafe.**

The Nervous System & Trauma Responses

When we develop **survival beliefs**, they manifest through the body's **four main trauma responses:**

- **Fight** – Becoming overly controlling, reactive, or aggressive as a way to protect yourself.
- **Flight** – Constant busyness, overworking, or avoiding emotional discomfort.
- **Freeze** – Feeling stuck, dissociating, or struggling to take action.
- **Fawn** – People-pleasing, prioritising others' needs over your own, or struggling with boundaries.

Each of these responses **originated as protection**. But as adults, they can **keep us trapped** in outdated coping mechanisms that no longer serve us.

24

Belinda's Personal Story: The Perfectionism Narrative

"If I do everything right, I'll be safe."

For years, I carried the belief that **my worth was tied to my ability to perform, succeed, and be everything to everyone.**

Growing up, I learned that **being productive, self-sufficient, and competent** was the only way to be accepted. Resting felt weak. Asking for help felt shameful. The story I internalised was simple: *"If I work hard enough, I will be safe."*

This belief **ruled my life.** I pushed myself beyond exhaustion, ignored my body's warning signs, and constantly sought validation through achievement. I was seen as "capable" and "strong," but I was actually drowning inside and I was depleted on many levels.

Then, during a personal development retreat, I was put on display as an example of **unhealthy patterns—without warning.** It felt like betrayal. I felt attacked, belittled, embarrassed and incredibly hurt. But it was also **the moment my story cracked open.**

For the first time, I saw how deeply **my nervous system had been wired to survive, not thrive.** The endless work, the burnout cycles, the not trusting myself, the inability to rest—these were **not personality traits. They were trauma responses.** For the first time I also realised some of the therapy I'd done previously had been retraumatising me.

The moment I stopped asking "What's wrong with me?" and started asking "What happened to me?", everything changed.

The Stories We Carry

Here are examples of how unconscious stories can shape our lives:

- **The Overachiever** – Raised in an environment where love was tied to success, they push relentlessly, fearing failure means rejection.
- **The Caretaker** – Growing up with emotionally unavailable parents, they learned that tending to others' needs is the only way to be valued.
- **The Invisible One** – After being repeatedly ignored or dismissed as a child, they now struggle to speak up, fearing they don't matter.
- **The One Who Can't Rest** – Witnessing caregivers struggle financially or emotionally, they believe relaxation is dangerous or selfish.

Each of these patterns was once **adaptive**. But now, they keep us in **cycles of stress, burnout, and self-abandonment**.

Practical Exercises: Rewriting the Narrative

Exercise 1: Identifying Your Core Beliefs

Journal Prompt: *"What is one belief I have about myself that keeps me stuck?"* (e.g., *"I must earn love,"* *"I can't trust others,"* *"I'm not enough")*

Exercise 2: Tracking Emotional Responses

Body Awareness: Notice what happens in your body when you challenge an old belief. Do you tense up? Feel anxious? This is your nervous system **resisting change**. Acknowledge it without judgment.

Exercise 3: A More Supportive Story

Reframe: Instead of affirmations, ask: *"What is a more supportive belief that my nervous system can accept?"* (e.g., *"It is safe for me to rest,"* *"I am allowed to take up space")*

Your Story Can Change

The stories you carry were **not chosen by you**—they were shaped by experience, survival, and adaptation. But the good news is:

You have the power to rewrite them.

Your brain can rewire. Your nervous system can regulate. Your identity can evolve. And every small shift brings you closer to your **authentic self. This is the work of becoming real.**

Chapter 3: Rewiring & Reconnecting with Your True Self

"You can't think your way into a new way of living. You have to live your way into a new way of thinking."
– Richard Rohr

Rewiring Old Patterns, Reclaiming Your Authenticity

By this stage, you've begun peeling back the layers—seeing the masks, roles, and beliefs that have shaped your identity. You've explored how trauma, conditioning, and survival patterns have influenced your **thoughts, behaviours, and nervous system responses**. Now, it's time to move from **awareness to transformation**.

Rewiring and reconnecting isn't about forcing change or using willpower. It's about:

- **Learning how the brain and nervous system rewire** so that change becomes sustainable.
- **Creating a felt sense of safety** so your body and mind can accept a new way of being.
- **Identifying the small, daily shifts** that reinforce authenticity in a way that feels natural.
- **Reclaiming your ability to trust yourself**—your intuition, emotions, and inner wisdom.

The goal isn't to erase who you've been—it's to **return to who you've always been underneath all of that conditioning.**

By the end of this chapter, you'll understand **how to disrupt old neural patterns and create new ones**, allowing your authentic self to emerge with greater ease and confidence.

The Science of Rewiring: Neuroplasticity & Nervous System Healing

For decades, neuroscience believed that the brain was **fixed and unchangeable** after childhood. We now know that the brain is **malleable, adaptable, and constantly reshaping itself** based on our experiences, thoughts, and behaviours. This process is called **neuroplasticity**.

How Change Happens in the Brain

When you repeatedly think a thought, feel an emotion, or engage in a behaviour, your brain strengthens those neural pathways. The more you reinforce an identity (*"I have to be perfect to be worthy"*), the more it becomes an **automatic pattern**.

To change this, you need to:

1. **Interrupt the old pattern** (awareness and emotional regulation).
2. **Introduce a new, more supportive belief** (subconscious reprogramming and somatic work).
3. **Repeat the new behaviour until it becomes your new default** (practice and integration).

But here's the key: **Your nervous system must feel safe enough to accept the change.**

If your **body still perceives authenticity as dangerous** —if setting boundaries, slowing down, or speaking your truth triggers fear—you will unconsciously resist change.

That's why healing is not just about the mind— it's about the body.

Belinda's Personal Story: Learning to Trust Myself Again

"For so long, I outsourced my decisions to others because I didn't trust myself to get it right."

After years of living in survival mode, I realised I had **completely lost touch with my own voice**. I constantly sought external validation—was I doing enough? Was I making the right choices? Did others approve of me?

When I started my healing journey, I thought change would be simple: **Just decide to be different.** *"Make a different choice"* is what I'd been told over and over.

But my body had other plans.

Whenever I tried to slow down, rest, or make decisions based on my own needs, I felt **a deep sense of unease**. It was as if my entire system screamed, *"This is unsafe!"*

I now understand this was my **nervous system resisting change and it played a strong game!** My brain was wired to believe that self-sacrifice, overachievement, and putting others first were the only ways to be safe and loved. Choosing myself felt like a threat.

The breakthrough came when I realised: **Healing isn't about convincing myself to change—it's about showing my body that change is safe.**

I started with small, tangible shifts:

- **Pausing before responding to others**, asking myself, *"What do I actually want?"* (And I also had to give myself permission to want it and remind myself that I was safe).
- **Using different somatic grounding techniques** when discomfort arose, instead of reacting. (Taking my awareness into my heart or going down into my body, did not feel safe for me so I needed external options for resourcing).
- **Speaking my truth in low-stakes situations** before tackling bigger challenges.

Very slowly, my nervous system **began to trust me again**. And the more I practiced, the more natural it felt to **live in alignment with my true self**. This process also really triggered some people in my life.

How Rewiring Can Look Different for Everyone

- **The Overthinker:** Learns to shift from constant analysis to trusting their intuitive decisions.
- **The People-Pleaser:** Moves from seeking approval to feeling safe expressing their true needs.
- **The Avoider:** Replaces numbing behaviours with emotional regulation tools that actually work.
- **The Perfectionist:** Let's go of control and embraces imperfection without fear of failure.

Every healing journey is different. The goal is to find what works **for your nervous system, your life, and your truth. Find your balance.**

Practical Exercises: Rewiring & Reconnecting

Exercise 1: Reclaiming Your Intuition

Journal Prompt: *"When have I ignored my intuition in the past? What happened? How did I feel in my body?" (Numbness is also a feeling).*

Try This: Spend one day making **small decisions** based purely on gut instinct (what to eat, what route to take, when to rest) and notice how it feels.

Exercise 2: The Nervous System Reset

Grounding Practice: Place one hand on your heart and one on your belly. Take **slow, deep breaths that reach deep down into your belly**, repeating: *"It is safe for me to be in my body. I am safe. I am safe. I am safe"*

Exercise 3: Interrupting Old Patterns

Reframe: When you catch yourself in an old thought loop (*"I should be doing more"*), pause and ask: *"What would my authentic self say instead?"*

You Can Trust Yourself Again

Rewiring and reconnecting is a process of **building self-trust, one small choice at a time.**

You don't have to transform overnight. You don't have to force change. And you don't have to do something that someone else told you to do. Your job is to pay attention and create **small, daily moments where your body and mind learn that authenticity is safe.**

Each time you:

- Choose rest over hustle,
- Speak your truth instead of shrinking back,
- Follow your gut instead of seeking approval,

You send a message to your nervous system: **I am safe to be me.** And over time, that becomes your new reality.

Pause and notice the weight of your body, the sensation of your breath.

You are here and right now, you do not need to force anything. Just become aware of it.

Chapter 4: Integration – Living Authentically & Building Emotional Strength

"You do not just wake up and become the butterfly. Growth is a process." – Rupi Kaur

Bringing It All Together

By this stage, you have done the deep work of **recognising your masks, rewriting limiting stories, and beginning the process of rewiring your nervous system.** Now, the focus shifts to **integration**—how to take this work and make it part of your daily life.

Healing is not just about uncovering what's been hidden; it's about **creating a new way of being that feels natural, sustainable, and deeply aligned with your true self.**

This chapter is about learning how to embody authenticity in a way that is not performative but **rooted in deep emotional strength and courage.**

In this chapter, we will explore:

1. What it actually means to **live authentically,** beyond self-awareness.
2. How to **build emotional strength** so that authenticity becomes effortless rather than exhausting.
3. **Navigating the resistance** that comes up when stepping into a new identity.
4. How to develop **inner emotional safety** before we even begin setting boundaries externally.

The goal is to ensure that you don't just **understand these concepts intellectually**—you begin to **live them fully and unapologetically.**

The Process of Authentic Living: Beyond Awareness

Living authentically is not about:

- Trying to be a **different person overnight.**
- **Forcing yourself to be vulnerable** without emotional safety.
- **Expecting your relationships, work, or environment to immediately align** with your growth.

Instead, it's about **learning how to trust yourself again.**

- **Authenticity is a practice.** It's built in small, daily decisions.
- **Healing is layered.** Growth is cyclical, not linear.
- **Emotional safety comes first.** Before setting boundaries with others, we must learn how to **be with ourselves.**

This chapter is about **building the inner emotional scaffolding** that allows you to embody your truth without constantly second-guessing, seeking permission, or fearing rejection.

Belinda's Personal Story: Learning to Navigate Growth Without Self-Abandonment

"I thought healing meant becoming someone new. But I realised it was about remembering who I was before the world told me who to be."

For years, I did the **inner work**—therapy, self-reflection, breaking old habits. I had all the awareness, but when it came to actually **living differently**, I found myself slipping back into old patterns.

I would say no—and then feel guilty. I would express a boundary—then soften it if someone was uncomfortable. I would embrace rest—then shame myself for being unproductive.

What I didn't realise was that my **body was still catching up** to my mind. My nervous system was wired to **prioritise safety through people-pleasing and overworking**, so every time I tried to do something different, it **felt wrong—even when I knew it was right.**

The shift happened when I started **building emotional empowerment and strength, not just self-awareness. I stopped seeing vulnerability and discomfort as weakness and failure,** and started seeing them as **a necessary step toward transformation.**

And I began saying the word 'no' a lot more, and I discovered that I really liked doing that.

The Emotional Challenges of Integration

- **The Fear of Backlash:** A person who starts expressing their truth but struggles with how others react due to the perceived and real actions and reactions.
- **The Discomfort of New Boundaries:** Someone who is learning to set limits but still battles the guilt and self-doubt that comes with it.
- **The Pushback from Old Circles:** A person whose growth is not well received by friends, family, or colleagues who preferred them in their old role.
- **The Resistance to Change Within:** Someone who is stepping into authenticity but feels overwhelmed by the fear of losing their identity in the process.

These struggles are **not signs that you are failing—** they are signs that you are **growing in a way that your body and mind need time to adjust to.**

You are allowed to take up space.

You are allowed to grow.

Also, never feel guilty about choosing to take care of yourself and your dependant children first.
A fully grown and evolved adult will never ask nor expect or guilt trip you into choosing an another adult over yourself or your offspring.

Practical Exercises: Building Emotional Strength

Exercise 1: The Authenticity Compass

Journal Prompt: "Where do I still hesitate to show up as my full self? What am I afraid will happen if I do?"

Try This: When making decisions, ask yourself, "Is this a choice made from my truth or from my fear?"

Exercise 2: Emotional Strength in Action

Somatic Practice: Sit with a moment of discomfort instead of immediately reacting. Notice where it sits in your body and just witness it. Name it. Breathe into it. Let it pass without needing to fix or change it.

Exercise 3: Identifying Your Emotional Anchors

Create a list of three things that can help you come back to yourself when you feel like you're slipping into old patterns. Some examples could be to ground yourself physically, splash cold water on your face, get up and stretch or text a supportive friend.

Transitioning to Emotional Resourcing: The Next Step in Growth

Before we can fully integrate authenticity, we must feel **safe within ourselves.** Many people make the mistake of thinking they need to set **external boundaries** first, but **in reality, we must first set internal boundaries with ourselves.**

- We must learn to **self-soothe before seeking validation.**
- We must know how to **hold space for our emotions** before expecting others to.
- We must feel **safe enough to expand** before expecting change to feel good.

This is why the next step of this journey is **emotional resourcing—learning how to create a deep, internal sense of safety so that authenticity becomes effortless rather than a constant battle.**

"I honour where I've been and trust where I am going."

Chapter 5: Emotional Resourcing – Creating an Inner Foundation of Safety

"We don't heal by thinking differently. We heal by feeling safe enough to experience life differently." – Dr. Gabor Maté

Building Emotional Safety from Within

Before true transformation can take place, your nervous system must feel **safe enough to change.** Emotional resourcing is the process of building an **internal sense of stability, grounding, and self-support** so that healing becomes sustainable, not just temporary.

Many people believe healing is about **letting go** or **moving on,** but in reality, it's about **creating enough internal safety to process what's been suppressed.** _If your body and mind don't feel safe, no amount of mindset shifts will stick._

In this chapter, we'll explore:

- What **emotional resourcing** is and why it's essential for deep healing.
- **Creating a personal emotional toolkit** to support you in moments of distress or activation.
- How to develop **inner safety, self-soothing, and self-regulation** skills.
- Why this is the **missing piece in most personal development approaches.**

By the end of this chapter, you'll have **practical tools** to navigate emotions with more courage and strength.... and less overwhelm.

The Role of Emotional Safety in Healing

Trauma and conditioning teach us to **prioritise external safety over internal safety.** We look to others for validation, security, and guidance—often at the expense of not listening to ourselves.

When we haven't developed internal emotional safety, we:

- Struggle to **regulate emotions** and feel overwhelmed easily.
- Seek **constant reassurance** from others instead of trusting ourselves.
- Feel **stuck in survival patterns** (fight, flight, freeze, fawn).
- Struggle to break cycles of **self-abandonment** or emotional numbing.

This is why healing is not just about **changing your thoughts**—it's about **teaching your body that it is safe to feel, express, and exist fully.**

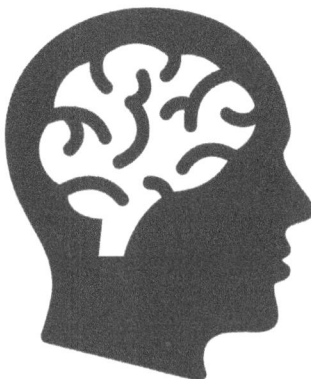

Belinda's Personal Story: Learning to Hold Myself First

"I spent years looking outside of myself for safety, never realising that what I needed was an internal foundation I had never built."

For so long, I believed that if I could just **do more, prove myself, and be who others needed me to be,** I would feel safe and secure. But no matter how much I achieved, I still felt like I was **one mistake away from everything falling apart.**

It wasn't until I started learning more about **emotional resourcing and nervous system regulation with a bottom up approach** that I realised—I had never really built a true internal foundation of safety. My entire sense of security was **external,** dependent on people's approval, my work performance, and my ability to hold everything together. I intellectualised and described what I was feeling instead of actually feeling it because it felt so unsafe in my body for me to feel, regardless of all the therapy I'd had.

The breakthrough came when I started asking myself:

- What if safety isn't something I have to earn?
- What if I can create a sense of safety within myself, no matter what happens externally?

For the first time, I began **practicing self-soothing, internal validation, and nervous system regulation.**

Very slowly, my sense of safety started shifting from external factors to something I carried within me. I also found inner child healing to be more effective than previous attempts.

How Emotional Resourcing Changes Lives

- **The Overwhelmed Empath** – Someone who absorbs others' emotions learns to create an internal boundary and develop emotional strength.
- **The Anxiety-Driven Perfectionist** – Learns how to self-soothe in moments of uncertainty rather than spiralling into overthinking.
- **The Abandonment Survivor** – Shifts from seeking constant reassurance to developing an inner sense of security and self-trust.
- **The High-Achiever Who Can't Rest** – Begins to feel safe slowing down, allowing joy and stillness to exist without guilt.

Practical Exercises: Developing Emotional Safety

Exercise 1: The Self-Soothing Practice

Journal Prompt: *"What makes me feel safe, grounded, and at peace? How can I cultivate more of that in my daily life?"*

Try This: Create a **personalised self-soothing ritual** (e.g., deep breathing, grounding, warm tea, calming music) for moments of distress.

Exercise 2: Anchoring in Safety

Body Awareness: Place one hand on your heart and the other on your belly. Breathe deeply and repeat: *"I am safe in this moment."*

Exercise 3: Building an Emotional Toolkit

Create a list of five things that help you regulate when you're feeling emotionally overwhelmed. Keep this list somewhere accessible for quick reference. (There is an emergency toolkit in a later chapter.)

You Are Your Own Safe Space

Safety isn't something you have to chase, earn, or seek from others.

It's something you can **build within yourself, moment by moment.**

You have the power to hold yourself, soothe yourself, and stand in your truth—even in moments of discomfort.

And that changes everything.

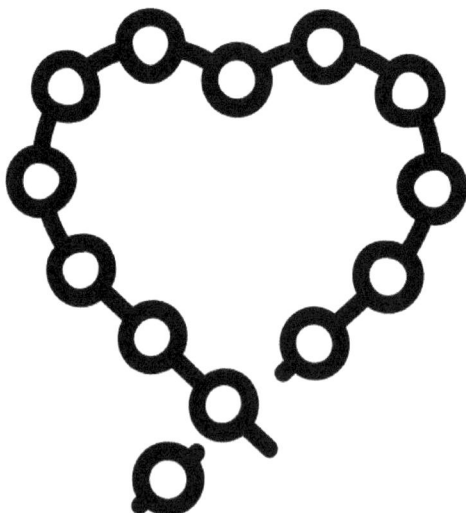

Gentle reminder:

Healing is not about fixing yourself -
You were never broken.

Now, take a deep breath.
There is no urgency.
You are safe in this moment.

Chapter 6: Processing Anger & Reclaiming Emotional Power

"Anger is not the enemy. It is the boundary, the warning, the call to action." – Unknown

Understanding Anger as a Messenger, Not a Threat

For many, anger is an emotion that has been **shamed, suppressed, or misunderstood**. Whether we were taught that anger is *dangerous, unproductive, or a sign of losing control*, many of us have been conditioned to either **deny it completely** or **let it consume us**.

But anger is **not the problem**—it's the **suppression or misdirection of anger** that creates dysfunction. When processed in a healthy way, anger is one of our **most powerful emotional tools** for transformation. It signals where boundaries have been crossed, where we have been harmed, and where we need to reclaim power.

In this chapter, we will explore:
* **Why anger is often suppressed**, especially in trauma survivors.
* **How unprocessed anger manifests in the body** and nervous system.
* **The difference between reactive anger and embodied anger.**
* **How to safely process anger** in a way that leads to empowerment.
* **Somatic practices for releasing stored anger without harm.**

By the end of this chapter, you will be able to **recognise, process, and harness anger as a tool for healing and personal strength.**

Why We Suppress Anger: Conditioning & Trauma

Many of us learned at a young age that anger was **not acceptable**. We were taught or heard:

→ *"Good people don't get angry."*
→ *"Don't cry or I'll give you something to cry about."*
→ *"Suck it up" or "Drink some cement and harden up"*
→ *"Anger makes you irrational or out of control."*
→ *"If you express anger, you will be rejected, punished, or abandoned."*
→ *"Go throw yourself into work to focus on something else."*
→ *"Go to timeout and think about what you've done" (as if you even knew how to process it)*

For trauma survivors, anger is often **intertwined with fear and survival responses**:

- If expressing anger was met with **punishment or neglect**, we learned to suppress it.
- If we witnessed **anger as destructive**, we vowed never to become that person.
- If our boundaries were **constantly crossed**, anger became internalised as self-criticism instead of an external expression.

The Impact of Caregiver Anger & Emotional Dysregulation on Childhood Development

Children who grow up in environments where **anger is explosive, unpredictable, or unsafe** often develop deep-rooted trauma responses that persist into adulthood.

When a caregiver has **unregulated emotions, substance abuse issues, or relies on punishment and reactivity instead of communication**, it creates an unstable emotional landscape.

If other caregivers in the home **appease or enable** the reactive caregiver rather than providing emotional safety, the child unconsciously learns that:

1. **Expressing their needs is dangerous**
2. **Speaking up leads to punishment, rejection, or shame.**
3. **Suppressing emotions is the safest way to survive.**

Over time, this results in **a fundamental disconnection from their emotional truth.** Because they were never given a **safe space to express and process emotions,** they grow up **without the tools to regulate anger in a healthy way.** Instead, anger becomes something to **fear, avoid, or turn inward.**

As adults, they **literally do not know another way of handling anger** because suppression, avoidance, or internalisation were the only coping mechanisms that ever felt safe.

Instead of recognising anger as a **healthy signal for boundaries, self-protection, and self-respect**, they may experience:

1. **A tendency to minimise their own feelings** to avoid conflict.
2. **Emotional numbing, dissociation, or self-sabotage** when faced with triggering situations.
3. **Deep sadness, guilt, or anxiety** in moments where anger would be appropriate.

*But the truth is: **Anger itself is not the problem. The absence of safe outlets for anger is.***

The Science: How Suppressed Anger Affects the Body & Mind

When anger is not processed, it doesn't just *go away* —it gets stored in the body and shows up as:

- **Chronic tension** (tight jaw, clenched fists, migraines, digestive issues).
- **Emotional outbursts** that seem disproportionate to the situation.
- **Passive-aggressive behaviours** or resentment that builds over time.
- **Depression or numbness,** as anger turns inward when it has no place to go.
- **Self-sabotage,** where anger gets redirected into unhealthy coping mechanisms, like addictions.

From a **nervous system perspective,** suppressed anger often keeps us in a **chronic fight, flight, freeze, or fawn** state:

- **Fight:** Reacting aggressively or lashing out when overwhelmed.
- **Flight:** Avoiding conflict and emotional confrontation.
- **Freeze:** Feeling stuck, unable to access the words or actions needed to stand up for oneself.
- **Fawn:** Prioritising others' comfort over expressing our own emotions.

The key to working with anger is not to **ignore it or explode with it**—it's about **learning to process and integrate it so it becomes a source of empowerment rather than destruction.**

Belinda's Personal Story: Uncovering the Layers of Suppressed Anger

"For years, I expressed sadness and frustration over the same things, never realising that underneath it all was unprocessed anger I had been taught to suppress."

Growing up, I learned that **children should be seen and not heard**. Speaking up—whether to express emotions, set a boundary, or question authority—was often met with **punishment, dismissal, or shame**. The safest thing to do was **stay quiet, comply, and avoid conflict at all costs.**

As a child, I didn't have the emotional tools to process what this meant. I just knew that **being too much, needing too much, or expressing too much came with consequences**. So, I adapted. I learned to **stay small, agreeable, and easy**—a pattern that carried well into adulthood.

Because of this conditioning, I never allowed myself to feel **anger**. Instead, I felt **frustration, sadness, and helplessness**—the more "acceptable" emotions that masked what was actually underneath. Even as I worked through layers of healing, I found myself expressing the same frustrations over and over again, yet never fully moving past them, often feeling retraumatised instead.

It wasn't until I began working with **somatic healing and nervous system regulation** that I uncovered the deeper truth:

I wasn't just frustrated.
I wasn't just sad.
I was angry. Really angry.
Raging with anger actually.
And I was absolutely terrified of expressing it.
And I had been this way for a very, very long time.

For the first time, I saw my **repressed anger for what it really was**—a necessary, protective emotion that had been shut down for decades. As I allowed myself to explore this, I began to recognise **the ripple effect of that conditioning**—how it had shaped a **deep sense of insignificance, insecurity, unworthiness, and disappointment within myself.**

And with it came **looping patterns of judgment, rejection, abandonment, toxic shame and mistreatment.** These weren't isolated experiences; they were **intergenerational wounds**—patterns of **suppression, disempowerment, and unspoken pain** that had been passed down through generations and it was not gender specific.

For so long, I carried this weight, believing it was mine. **It wasn't.** It was the emotional inheritance of those who came before me—people who also never had the space to understand or process their own pain.

Once I learnt some deeper somatic resourcing tools that enabled me to feel safer within myself, I was able to shift the blockages and give myself permission to **acknowledge and process the anger and everything that came with it.** I found I could finally **break cycles that had followed me well into my 40s.**

Anger, when processed safely, became one of my **greatest allies in reclaiming my power.**

Empowering Message: Anger is a Call to Strength, Not Destruction

Anger, when processed and understood, is one of the most **powerful forces for self-protection and transformation.**

It is not an enemy—it is an **ally waiting to be acknowledged.**

When you stop fearing anger, you start learning from it. And when you learn from it, you begin reclaiming your **emotional power.**

Chapter 7: Breaking the Cycle of Self-Abandonment

"Every time you choose yourself over the patterns that once kept you small, you reclaim your power."
– Unknown

Understanding Self-Abandonment & The Path to Self-Trust

Self-abandonment happens when we repeatedly **dismiss our needs, silence our emotions, or prioritise external validation over our inner truth.** It is often so deeply ingrained that we don't even recognise when we are doing it.

This cycle doesn't begin in adulthood—it starts in childhood, when we learn that **our authenticity is not safe.** Whether through **subtle invalidation or outright neglect, trauma, or conditioning,** many of us internalised the belief that **who we truly are is not enough**—so we learned to **adapt, suppress, and perform** in order to feel accepted.

This chapter is about:

1. **Recognising the signs of self-abandonment** and how it manifests in relationships, career, and decision-making.
2. Understanding **how childhood experiences shaped your patterns of self-sacrifice.**
3. **Learning how to disrupt the cycle** and step into a space of self-honouring and self-trust.
4. **Practicing self-reconnection tools** to strengthen your sense of worth from within.

By the end of this chapter, you'll be able to identify where self-abandonment shows up in your life and take tangible steps toward reclaiming yourself.

How Self-Abandonment Begins: Childhood Imprints & Survival Adaptations

As children, we are wired for **connection and survival.** If a child grows up in an environment where **their emotions are dismissed, their needs are unmet, or their authenticity is punished,** they learn one thing: *It is safer to abandon myself than to risk being abandoned by others.*

This often looks like:

> Being the "easy child" who never causes problems.

> Learning to read others' emotions before expressing your own.

> Feeling responsible for keeping the peace.

> Shrinking or staying silent to avoid conflict.

> Overachieving to prove worth.

When these adaptations are carried into adulthood, they become **default patterns** that shape how we show up in relationships, work, and self-worth.

Signs You Are Engaging in Self-Abandonment

- **Ignoring Your Intuition** – Second-guessing yourself or needing outside validation to feel "right."
- **Neglecting or Dismissing Your Needs** – Prioritising everyone else while feeling exhausted, resentful, or depleted.
- **Saying Yes When You Want to Say No** – Avoiding conflict at the cost of your well-being.
- **Dismissing, Minimising or Disregarding Your Feelings** – Convincing yourself your emotions aren't "valid" or "big enough" to matter.
- **Over-functioning in Relationships** – Taking responsibility for others' emotions or constantly trying to "fix" people.
- **Overworking & Overachieving** – Linking your self-worth to money, productivity or external success.
- **Seeking Constant External Reassurance** – Feeling unable to trust your own decisions without approval from others.

The good news? **Self-abandonment is a learned survival response. That means it can be unlearned.**

Belinda's Personal Story: Realising the Depth of Self-Abandonment

"I didn't realise how much I had abandoned myself until I started choosing myself—and everything in me resisted it."

For most of my life, I convinced myself that **I was strong, independent, and didn't need much from others**. It was all I'd heard throughout my life as well, and I took it as a compliment.

What I didn't realise was that **my self-sufficiency was actually a trauma response**—a deeply ingrained habit of **not needing anything because I had learned early on that my needs wouldn't be met.**

I ignored my intuition, dismissing the quiet voice that told me when something wasn't right. I prioritised everyone else's emotions, ensuring I was likable, easy, and never a burden. I overworked, believing my worth was tied to how much I could give.

It wasn't until I started setting small boundaries that I realised just how deep my self-abandonment ran. **Every time I chose myself, I felt a wave of guilt and fear.** My body reacted as if choosing myself was dangerous.

That was when I understood:
I wasn't just changing habits. I was breaking generational cycles of self-sacrifice.

Then things got really interesting.

How Self-Abandonment Manifests in Daily Life

- **The Caregiver Who Can't Receive** – Always giving, yet feeling uncomfortable asking for or accepting support.
- **The Overachiever Who Feels Empty** – Seeking success, yet never feeling like it's enough.
- **The People-Pleaser in Relationships** – Ignoring personal needs to maintain connection, even when it's unhealthy.
- **The Person Who Can't Slow Down** – Associating stillness with unworthiness or fear of being left behind.

These patterns don't make you "bad" or "broken"—they are survival adaptations. The goal is not to judge them, but to **recognise and rewrite them.**

Practical Exercises: Rebuilding Self-Trust & Self-Connection

Exercise 1: Identifying Where You Self-Abandon

Journal Prompt: *"Where do I say yes when I want to say no? Where do I ignore my intuition? Where do I minimise my needs?"*

Try This: The next time you feel torn between yourself and others, pause. Ask: *"If I deeply trusted myself, what would I choose?"*

Exercise 2: Self-Reconnection Practice

Somatic Practice: Place a hand on your heart and say: *"I am here. I see you. I will not leave you again."* Notice any discomfort. Acknowledge it. Breathe through it.

Exercise 3: Choosing Yourself in Small Ways

Start small: Make **one decision today** that prioritises your own needs without explaining, justifying, or apologising.

You Are Allowed to Choose Yourself

Every time you choose yourself, you are breaking a cycle.

You are showing your nervous system that **you are safe to exist as you are.**

You are not here to abandon yourself, so others feel comfortable.

You are not here to perform, please, or prove your worth.

You are here to **stand fully in who you are.** And that is enough.

"Exhale slowly. Let go of tension. There is nothing you need to force right now."

Chapter 8: Healing Trauma Responses & Reclaiming Nervous System Safety

"Trauma is not what happens to you, but what happens inside you as a result of what happens to you." – Dr. Gabor Maté

Understanding Trauma Responses & Nervous System Healing

Healing is not just about changing your mindset—it's about **creating safety in your body** so that transformation is sustainable.

Many people attempt healing by focusing only on their thoughts, wondering why they keep **falling back into old habits, relationships, or emotional patterns.** But trauma doesn't live in the mind—it lives in the **nervous system**, shaping how we respond to stress, relationships, and even ourselves.

If you've ever felt **stuck, reactive, emotionally numb, or constantly on edge**, it's not because you're broken. It's because your nervous system is still operating from **old survival patterns.**

This chapter will explore:

> What trauma responses are and how they manifest in daily life.
> How the nervous system shapes our emotional and behavioural patterns.
> The difference between trauma triggers and trauma loops.
> Practical somatic tools to regulate the nervous system and create lasting change.

By the end of this chapter, you will have a **clear understanding of your nervous system's role in healing** and tangible techniques to move from survival mode to a state of safety and empowerment.

Understanding Trauma Responses:
Fight, Flight, Freeze & Fawn

Our nervous system is wired to **protect us from danger**. When we experience stress or trauma, the body reacts with a **survival response** designed to keep us safe. But if the trauma was never resolved, these responses can become **stuck**, influencing how we move through life.

The Four Main Trauma Responses

- **Fight** – Reacting with defensiveness, aggression, or control when feeling unsafe. (*"If I stay in control, I'll be safe."*)
- **Flight** – Avoiding discomfort by staying constantly busy or distracted. (*"If I keep moving, I won't have to feel."*)
- **Freeze** – Shutting down, dissociating, or feeling paralysed in response to stress. (*"If I become invisible, nothing bad will happen."*)
- **Fawn** – People-pleasing, over-explaining, or sacrificing personal needs to keep the peace. (*"If I keep everyone happy, I won't be rejected."*)

Each of these responses **began as a way to survive, like adaptation in our responses and behaviours, in order to keep us feeling safe**. The problem arises when they become our **default reactions**, keeping us stuck in cycles that no longer serve us.

How Trauma Responses Shape Your Life

The Fight Response:

- Difficulty trusting others or delegating.
- Needing control over situations, emotions, or people.
- Using anger or aggression as a defence mechanism.

The Flight Response:

- Constant busyness or overworking to avoid emotional discomfort.
- Feeling restless, anxious, or unable to slow down.
- Avoiding deep emotional connections or self-reflection.

The Freeze Response:

- Struggling to take action or make decisions.
- Feeling emotionally numb or disconnected from life.
- Experiencing brain fog or dissociation in stressful situations.

The Fawn Response:

- Struggling to say no or set boundaries.
- Prioritising others' emotions over your own.
- Feeling guilt or anxiety when asserting yourself.

Recognising these patterns is the **first step toward healing**. You are not "stuck" this way—your nervous system simply needs **new signals of safety.**

Belinda's Personal Story: Learning to Regulate My Nervous System

"I thought I was just an anxious person. I didn't realise my nervous system was still living in past trauma."

For years, I **overworked, overgave, and overexplained.** I stayed **busy** to avoid discomfort, I **shut down** when I felt overwhelmed, and I **prioritised other people's emotions over my own.**

I assumed this was just my personality—until I started learning about **trauma responses and nervous system dysregulation.** I realised that **my exhaustion, anxiety, and overthinking weren't personal failings—** they were survival patterns my body had adopted long ago.

Healing didn't come from forcing myself to "just relax" or repeating affirmations I didn't believe. Healing came once *I believed I was safe.* Then I started **teaching my nervous system that it was safe to slow down, safe to feel, and safe to exist without performing.**

For the first time, I wasn't trying to fix myself. I was learning how to **support myself in ways I had never been taught before.**

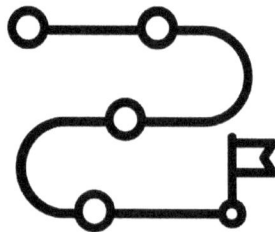

Recognising Trauma Patterns in Daily Life

The High-Functioning Flight Response – Someone who overworks, overcommits, and never stops moving to avoid discomfort.

The Freeze-Mode Shutdown – A person who struggles to take action, feeling overwhelmed by decisions or responsibilities.

The Fawn Response in Relationships – A caregiver who sacrifices their own needs, fearing rejection if they set boundaries.

The Fight Response as Hyper-Independence – Someone who avoids vulnerability, seeing it as weakness instead of strength.

Each of these patterns is **not who you are**—it's what your nervous system has learned. The good news? **It can learn something new.**

Practical Exercises: Rewiring the Nervous System for Safety

Exercise 1: Tracking Your Trauma Response Patterns

Journal Prompt: *"Which trauma response do I recognise in myself? How has it shaped my behaviours and relationships?"*

Try This: Notice when you feel activated. Label the response—*Is this fight, flight, freeze, or fawn?* Awareness is the first step to change.

Exercise 2: The Vagus Nerve Reset for Nervous System Healing

Somatic Practice:

- Inhale deeply for **four seconds,** hold for **four seconds,** and exhale slowly for **six seconds.**
- Gently hum or sing to activate the **vagus nerve,** signalling safety to the nervous system.
- Place a hand on your chest and repeat: *"I am safe in this moment."*

Exercise 3: Creating a Daily Nervous System Regulation Practice

Design a simple ritual that helps your body return to a state of calm—this could be grounding exercises, movement, or mindful breathing.

You Are Not Your Trauma Responses

Your trauma responses are not personality traits. They are **adaptations that kept you safe.**

But safety can now look different.

It can look like ease, stillness, and connection.
It can look like slowing down without guilt.
It can look like trusting your own voice and honouring your needs.

The goal is not to get rid of your nervous system's instincts—it's to **teach your body that it is safe to choose differently.**

And with time, it will.

Chapter 9: Navigating Setbacks & Relapse – How to Handle Difficult Moments

"Healing is not about never falling back into old patterns. It's about noticing when you do and choosing differently, again and again."
– Unknown

Why Setbacks Happen & How to Handle Them with Compassion

One of the **biggest myths** about healing is that once you "**do the work,**" you **never struggle again.** In reality, **healing is cyclical, not linear.** Setbacks are not failures —they are part of the process.

Relapse into old habits, survival responses, or self-abandonment **does not mean you are "back at square one.**" It means your nervous system is seeking familiarity in times of stress.

The key is not to avoid setbacks altogether—it's learning how to move through them with **awareness, self-compassion, and understanding.**

Healing is like peeling back the layers of an onion. Each time you think you've worked through something, a new layer appears—offering deeper insight, new challenges, and more profound transformation.

Just because you encounter an **old wound doesn't mean you haven't grown.** It simply means there's another layer ready to be **acknowledged and healed.**

This chapter will explore:

1. **Why setbacks happen** and how to reframe them as growth opportunities.
2. **How to recognise early signs of emotional or behavioural relapse.**
3. **Understanding shame spirals and toxic shame,** and how to break free from them.
4. **Practical strategies to self-regulate and realign** after a difficult moment.
5. **How to build a personal action plan for handling challenges,** including an emergency grounding toolkit.

By the end of this chapter, you will have a toolkit for navigating setbacks with confidence, without falling into shame or self-sabotage.

Why Setbacks Are Normal in Healing

Healing is not a straight path. Just like physical recovery, emotional recovery involves moments of strength and moments of challenge. Many people experience relapse into old patterns when they:

1. Face a triggering situation that activates old emotional wounds.
2. Feel overwhelmed, stressed, or emotionally exhausted.
3. Encounter relationships or environments that reinforce past conditioning.
4. Struggle with self-doubt or fear of outgrowing their past identity.
5. Experience major life changes that unsettle their sense of stability.

In these moments, the nervous system defaults to what it knows best—even if those habits or coping mechanisms no longer serve you. **And sometimes, the hardest thing to recognise is that numbness is still a feeling.**

*Many trauma survivors **dismiss their own experience** because **they don't feel anything at all.** But **emotional shutdown and numbness is just as much a response** as anxiety or anger—it's simply the **body's way of managing overwhelm.***

Shame Spirals & Toxic Shame: How They Keep You Stuck

Shame is one of the most paralysing emotions when it comes to healing. Unlike **guilt** (which is about feeling bad for something you did), shame is about feeling bad for who you are.

Toxic shame tells us:

"I am unworthy because I messed up."

"I'll never change. I always fall back into old patterns."

"I am too broken to heal."

This kind of self-talk creates a cycle of self-abandonment—one where **we punish ourselves instead of offering the kindness and patience**, we would extend to anyone else. **Shame thrives in secrecy.** The way out of a shame spiral is **awareness, self-compassion, and connection.**

How to Identify When You're Slipping into Old Patterns

- **Feeling disconnected from yourself** – Ignoring intuition, suppressing emotions, or losing touch with your needs.
- **Self-sabotaging behaviours returning** – Avoiding healing practices, overworking, numbing emotions, or isolating.
- **Reverting to people-pleasing or over-explaining** – Feeling the need to justify boundaries or accommodate others at your own expense.
- **Increased emotional reactivity** – Feeling more easily triggered, overwhelmed, or stuck in emotional loops.
- **Inner critic getting louder** – Experiencing thoughts of "I'm failing" or "I haven't changed at all."

Recognising these signs early can help you shift before you spiral into shame or hopelessness.

Belinda's Personal Story: Learning to Trust the Process, Even in Setbacks

"I thought healing meant never struggling again. I didn't realise the real healing was in how I handled the struggle."

I used to believe that once I healed, I would never feel **overwhelmed, triggered, or reactive** again. But every time I found myself falling back into self-doubt, over-explaining, or shutting down emotionally, **I felt like I had failed.**

What I didn't understand then was that **relapse wasn't failure—it was feedback.** It was my nervous system telling me I needed more support, more rest, or deeper self-trust.... and that was after I learnt that there was also a **difference between feedback and criticism.**

All feedback was criticism in my eyes prior to that as I literally was not aware that there was any distinction. **Some saw it as being in victim mode** however, you don't know what you don't know and when your entire life has been a trauma response, you literally do not know any different until you learn or are shown.

That was when a big lightbulb went off for me. The moment I **stopped judging myself** for slipping back into old habits was the moment I started truly healing. Because **healing isn't about perfection—it's about learning how to return to yourself, over and over again.**

In my case, I had to discover who I was authentically first, which takes time, and an immense amount of patience and compassion.

Emergency Grounding Toolkit: How to Bring Yourself Back to the Present Moment

When a setback happens, the most important thing is to regulate your nervous system quickly and reconnect with the present moment. Here are a few tools to use when needed. Try them all then choose which ones resonate with you:

- **5-4-3-2-1 Grounding Method** – Name 5 things you can see, 4 things you can touch, 3 things you can hear, 2 things you can smell, and 1 thing you can taste.
- **Vagus Nerve Activation** – Humming, singing, or placing a hand on your heart and taking deep breaths stimulates the vagus nerve, helping to shift you out of fight-or-flight.
- **Shake It Out** – Stand up and shake your hands, arms, and legs. This releases stored stress and tension from the body.
- **Cold Water Therapy** – Splashing cold water on your face or holding an ice cube can quickly bring your nervous system back to the present.
- **Body Compression** – Cross your arms and press your hands into your shoulders or thighs. This can create a sense of safety and containment.

Progress Is Measured by How You Return to Yourself

Healing is not about never slipping up. It's about learning how to come back to yourself with **kindness instead of self-judgment.** Each time you recognise an old pattern and choose differently—even if it's just a small shift—**you are rewiring your brain, healing your nervous system, and strengthening self-trust.** And that is the real definition of growth.

Chapter 10: Healing the Mother & Father Wounds – Releasing Generational Trauma

"You do not have to carry what was never yours to hold." – Unknown

Understanding the Parent Wound & Generational Trauma

Many of the patterns we struggle with—**self-worth issues, difficulty setting boundaries, emotional repression, fear of abandonment, or deep-seated shame—did not begin with us.** They were shaped by the caregivers who raised us, and in many cases, by the generations that came before them.

The mother and father wounds refer to **unresolved emotional pain, unmet needs, and conditioning we inherit from our parents or primary caregivers.** These wounds can manifest in both **overt and subtle ways,** shaping how we see ourselves, how we engage in relationships, and how safe we feel in the world.

But what if these patterns are all we've ever known?

Many people do not recognise they are carrying mother and father wounds because they don't have a frame of reference for anything different. If we were raised in an **emotionally unstable, avoidant, or inconsistent environment, our nervous system normalises that experience. It becomes our baseline.**

This is why we repeat patterns unknowingly—until we begin questioning the root of our struggles.

This chapter will explore:

- What mother and father wounds are and how they impact our **subconscious programmming and sense of self.**
- The ways **generational trauma** plays out in family dynamics.
- How these wounds **manifest in adulthood** and how they shape our attachment styles and relationship patterns.
- The process of releasing inherited pain and reclaiming your own identity.
- The **adaptations and coping mechanisms** we develop to survive these wounds.
- A guided practice for returning energy to its original sender with compassion and consciousness.

By the end of this chapter, you will understand how to release the emotional burdens that were never yours to carry and step into the freedom of your truth.

This is a really significant and transformational chapter. Be willing to give yourself permission and the space and with mindful curiosity and compassion, do some deep reflection on your mother and father wounds.

It is a game changer for so many people.

It's important to note: These wounds **do not mean** our parents or primary caregivers were "bad" people.

In most cases, they were simply **passing down the pain they never had the tools to heal.**

The Role of Generational Trauma

We don't just inherit physical traits from our family—we also inherit **beliefs, behaviours, and unprocessed emotional pain.**

- If past generations lived in **survival mode,** we may have learned that **rest is dangerous or that love must be earned through hard work and suffering.**
- If emotional suppression was the norm, we may have been taught to **minimise our feelings** or feel guilt for having needs.
- If past generations suffered **abandonment, war, financial instability, or oppression,** we may unconsciously carry **fear-based beliefs around safety, relationships, and self-worth.**

This is how **trauma becomes inherited.** And unless we consciously **break these cycles,** we will continue to pass them forward.

What Are the Mother & Father Wounds?

The Mother Wound – Emotional pain passed down through the maternal lineage, often manifesting as:

- Feeling **responsible for others' emotions** or struggling with over-nurturing.
- Believing **self-sacrifice is required for love**.
- Fear of being **too much or not enough**.
- Deep feelings of **guilt, shame, or unworthiness**.
- Difficulty **trusting other women** or struggling with **feminine energy (regardless of gender)**.

This wound **often stems from a mother** who was either **emotionally unavailable, hypercritical, overprotective, or enmeshed**. In many cases, the mother herself **was not given the space to heal**, and she unconsciously passed down her pain.

The Father Wound – Emotional pain stemming from the paternal lineage, often manifesting as:

- Struggles with **self-worth, validation, or feeling "good enough."**
- Fear of **rejection or abandonment in relationships**.
- Difficulty setting boundaries or asserting needs.
- Feeling **unsupported, unseen, or emotionally disconnected**.
- A deep-seated **fear of failure or pressure to achieve**.

This wound **often stems from a father** who was **emotionally distant, overly critical, absent, or unpredictable**. Whether through neglect, avoidance, or unrealistic expectations, the child **internalises the belief that love is conditional.**

Attachment Styles & Relationship Patterns

The way we bond with caregivers in childhood shapes our attachment patterns in adulthood. **These attachment styles influence how we form and maintain relationships, respond to emotional needs, and navigate intimacy.** People may have traits from multiple styles depending on their life experiences.

Secure Attachment → Develops when emotional needs were consistently met → Leads to healthy communication, trust, and emotional regulation.

Anxious Attachment → Develops when love was inconsistent → Leads to fear of abandonment, need for reassurance, emotional highs/lows.

Dismissive-Avoidant Attachment → Develops when caregivers were emotionally unavailable or dismissive → Leads to emotional detachment, avoidance of intimacy, and over-reliance on independence.

Fearful-Avoidant Attachment (Disorganised Attachment) → Develops in chaotic, abusive, or inconsistent caregiving environments → Leads to push-pull dynamics, fear of both closeness and rejection.

Anxious-Avoidant Attachment → Develops when a person experiences both inconsistent love and emotional neglect → Leads to cycles of pursuit and withdrawal, alternating between craving connection and pushing it away.

When **mother and father wounds are unhealed,** we often **recreate** these attachment patterns in friendships, romantic relationships, and even work dynamics. They do not define who we are but they can shape how we relate to others until we become aware of them.

How the Mother & Father Wounds Manifest in Daily Life

When a person has **never known a reality outside of their wounds,** they develop **adaptations** that help them **survive** but later keep them stuck, known as coping mechanisms and trauma adaptations.

These include:

- **People-Pleasing & Overgiving** – Feeling responsible for others' happiness, struggling to say no. (Learned as a survival tactic to avoid rejection.)
- **Fear of Abandonment** – Staying in unhealthy relationships, tolerating mistreatment, or self-sabotaging before we can be rejected.
- **Struggles with Self-Worth** – Feeling unworthy of love, success, or ease unless we "earn" it through hardship.
- **Repeating Unhealthy Relationship Patterns** – Attracting emotionally unavailable partners or friendships that mirror parental dynamics.
- **Difficulty Feeling Emotionally Safe** – Struggling with trust, vulnerability, or expressing emotions openly.
- **Hyper-Independence** - A defense mechanism to avoid being let down by others.
- **Emotional Numbing & Dissociation** - A response to childhood overwhelm and overstimulation.

These patterns **do not mean we are broken**. They are **learned responses**. And what has been learned can be unlearned.

It is important to realise that whilst we may not be responsible for what happened to us, we are 100% responsible for doing the healing work.

Belinda's Personal Story: Releasing the Weight of Generational Pain

"For most of my life, I carried pain that wasn't mine. I took on the wounds of my family as if they were my responsibility to fix. But healing doesn't mean holding onto what was never yours to carry."

For years, I didn't realise that many of the struggles I faced—**self-doubt, guilt, emotional over-responsibility—were not entirely mine.** They were patterns that had been passed down through my family for generations.

I saw the same cycles in my mother and grandmother—the same struggles with self-worth, the same difficulty setting boundaries, the same unspoken grief. **Unprocessed pain moves through families until someone is ready to feel it, process it, and release it.**

The hardest part of healing wasn't acknowledging these wounds—it was realising that I had the power to **break the cycle.** That I could choose differently. That I didn't have to carry this weight any longer.

And as challenging as it has been, that has been the most liberating part of my journey.

Practical Process: Releasing Parent Wound & Returning Energy with Compassion

It is not your job to carry what was never yours to hold.

The following practice allows you to **return energy to its original sender** while honouring what was passed down with **consciousness and compassion.**

Step 1: Acknowledge the Inherited Pain

Journal Prompt: *"What struggles do I carry that I can see reflected in my parents or ancestors?"*

Try This: Reflect on what wounds may have been passed down, without judgment and without censoring yourself.

Step 2: Returning the Energy to Its Original Source Guided Visualisation:

- Find a quiet space. Close your eyes and take slow deep breaths, imagining yourself **holding the emotional burdens you've inherited.**
- Picture **your ancestors standing before you—** the ones who unknowingly passed these struggles down.
- Imagine or visualise gently placing the pain, beliefs, or emotional burdens into a **symbolic container.**
- Say (silently or aloud): *"I see the pain, conditioning, and survival patterns that were given to me. I recognise that they did not start with me. I release what is not mine with love. I send this energy back to its original owner with compassion and consciousness, knowing I no longer need to carry what is not mine and I am free to walk my own path."*
- Imagine or **visualise handing the symbolic object back to them** and the energy **leaving your body** and returning to its original source, while you remain whole and at peace. As you do it, say (silently or aloud): *"I release this with love. I no longer need to carry what is not mine."*
- **Call back your own energy.** Imagine a golden light returning to your body as you say silently or out aloud: *"I am free to create a new story. I honour what was, but choose what is mine to keep. Please return my own positive energy and all of the amazing good that is my birthright to me, cleansed, cleared and transmuted into good clean, loving abundant energy, and restored to its rightful place within me. Thank you"*
- Take a long, slow, mindful and refreshing breath.

Affirmation Practice:

- "I am not responsible for carrying the unhealed pain of my family."
- "I choose to break the cycle and walk a new path that is genuine and authentic for me."
- "I release with loving kindness, and I move forward with peace."

You Are Free to Walk Your Own Path

You do not have to hold onto what does not belong to you.

You are allowed to heal in ways your ancestors never could.

You are allowed to feel joy, ease, and freedom—without guilt.

Breaking cycles is not betrayal. It is liberation.
And you are worthy of it.

By doing this work, you are breaking cycles that have existed for generations. You are not just healing for yourself—you are changing what will be passed forward.

Chapter 11: Reconnecting with Joy, Play & Inner Freedom

"Healing isn't just about addressing pain. It's also about remembering how to feel joy." – Unknown

Rediscovering Playfulness & the Ability to Experience Joy

Trauma often teaches us that **life is about survival, not about joy.** Many people healing from trauma, burnout, or emotional suppression struggle to reconnect with feelings of **happiness, playfulness, and lightness** because their nervous system has been wired for **hyper-vigilance, responsibility, and self-protection.**

But **joy is not frivolous—it is a vital part of our emotional health.** Learning to experience **pleasure, creativity, and play** is just as important as processing pain.

This chapter will explore:

- Why joy can feel unsafe after trauma and how to gently reclaim it.
- The role of play in emotional regulation and healing.
- How perfectionism and hyper-responsibility block us from fun.
- Practical exercises to awaken joy and reconnect with the inner child.

By the end of this chapter, you will understand how **joy is a necessary and natural part of healing—**and that you are worthy of experiencing it.

Why Joy Can Feel Uncomfortable After Trauma

When we spend years in **fight, flight, freeze, or fawn mode**, our nervous system becomes accustomed to stress as the default state. Many trauma survivors:

- Feel **anxious when things are "too good"** because their body expects something bad to happen.
- Struggle to feel **present in joyful moments,** fearing they won't last.
- Associate **play and fun with irresponsibility or immaturity.**
- Feel **guilt when prioritizing pleasure or rest.**

But joy is not a luxury—it is a birthright. The key is to **reintroduce it slowly, in ways that feel safe and natural.**

The Role of Play in Healing

Playfulness is one of the **most powerful forms of nervous system regulation.** It allows us to **shift out of survival mode, release stored stress, and access creativity and spontaneity.**

As children, we **explored the world through curiosity, movement, and imagination.** But many of us lost that connection due to:

- Childhood environments that discouraged play or self-expression.
- Being forced into responsibility too young.
- Perfectionism that made us feel we had to "earn" fun.
- A focus on productivity that devalues rest and creativity.

Belinda's Personal Story: Learning to Experience Joy Without Guilt

"For years, I associated joy with irresponsibility. Fun was something I had to earn, not something I was inherently worthy of."

I didn't realise how much I had disconnected from **play, laughter, and creativity** until I was asked, *"What do you do for fun?"* And I had no answer.

For most of my life, I saw myself as **the responsible one**. I worked hard, took care of others, and carried the emotional weight of those around me. I believed that **joy was something you had to work for, not something you could just allow yourself to feel.**

The first time I let myself play—truly play, without guilt—I felt an unfamiliar mix of emotions. Excitement, nostalgia, and relief. But also, discomfort. **My nervous system wasn't used to joy feeling safe.**

Relearning how to experience lightness took time. I had to teach myself that **happiness wasn't dangerous, that I didn't have to prove my worth before allowing myself rest, and that play wasn't wasted time—it was healing.**

Relearning how to play is not childish.
It is one of the most advanced forms of healing.

How Reclaiming Playfulness Changes Lives

- **The Workaholic Who Never Learned to Rest** – Learns how to experience joy without guilt or feeling unproductive.
- **The Over-Responsible Caregiver** – Rediscovers creativity and personal passions that were long neglected.
- **The Perfectionist Who Struggles with Fun** – Learns to engage in activities without needing to excel or achieve.
- **The Highly Sensitive Person Who Over-analyses** – Reconnects with light-heartedness and experiences life with more ease.

These transformations don't happen overnight, but each small moment of joy **rewires the nervous system to expect ease instead of only stress.**

Practical Exercises: Reawakening Joy & Playfulness

Exercise 1: Reintroducing Play in Small Ways

Journal Prompt: *"What brought me joy as a child? (Or what can I imagine would have brought me joy as a child?)*

How can I incorporate a version of that into my life today?"

Try This: Make a list of **three small, playful activities** you can try this week (painting, dancing, playing an instrument, doing something silly just for fun).

Exercise 2: The Joy Inventory

Reflection Practice:

- Close your eyes and **visualise a moment when you felt completely free, joyful, or playful.**
- Notice how it feels in your body—**warmth, expansion, lightness.**
- Ask yourself: *"How can I bring more of this feeling into my daily life?"*

Exercise 3: Permission to Feel Joy

Self-Compassion Practice: If joy feels uncomfortable, remind yourself:

- "I am allowed to feel happy without guilt."
- "I do not have to earn rest, play, or fun."
- "Joy is a natural part of my healing process."

You Are Allowed to Feel Joy

Joy is not something you have to prove you deserve.

It is not something you have to wait for permission to experience.

It is something you can **choose to welcome back into your life, one small step at a time.**

Your healing journey is not just about processing pain —it is also about reclaiming **your ability to feel alive.**

Chapter 12: The Future Self – Embodying Your Highest Potential

"The version of you that you are becoming is already within you. Your job is to remove what is no longer aligned so they can emerge." – Unknown

Stepping Into the Next Version of Yourself

After peeling back the layers of conditioning, survival responses, and generational trauma, the most important question remains: **Who are you, now that you are no longer bound by the past?**

This chapter is about moving forward—not just intellectually, but **emotionally, energetically, and in action.** Your **future self already exists within you—** they are simply waiting for you to create the space for them to emerge.

This chapter will explore:

- How to envision and embody your future self.
- How to shift identity from survival-based thinking to expansive living.
- The role of embodiment in creating lasting transformation.
- A guided process to align your daily life with your highest potential.
- Releasing attachments to old identities with grace.

By the end of this chapter, you will have a clear **vision, mindset, and embodied practice** for stepping fully into your authentic self and highest potential.

The Power of Identity: Shifting Into a New Way of Being

Many people approach healing by trying to **fix** themselves. But **real transformation comes when we shift identity**—when we stop focusing on what we need to change and instead ask: **Who am I becoming?**

- If you have always identified as the caregiver, who are you when you put yourself first?
- If you have always identified as the overachiever, who are you when you don't need external validation?
- If you have always identified as the survivor, who are you when you are no longer in survival mode?

Healing is not just about what you let go of—it's about what you allow yourself to step into.

Breaking Free from the Fear of Expansion

Many people subconsciously fear their own transformation because:

- Growth requires stepping into the unknown.
- Success requires self-trust, which may feel unfamiliar.
- Thriving requires letting go of old identities that once kept you safe.

This is why self-sabotage often appears when things start getting better. Your **nervous system is wired for what is familiar**, even if that familiar space is pain, struggle, or limitation. **The key is to teach your body that expansion is safe.**

Belinda's Personal Story: Learning to Fully Step Into My Future Self

"I kept waiting for the 'right moment' to become the person I wanted to be. I didn't realise that the only thing standing between me and my future self was my own hesitation to step forward."

For years, I did the healing work, but I still found myself **feeling stuck at a threshold.** I had let go of the survival patterns, the self-abandonment, and the conditioning—but I didn't know what came next.

What I didn't realise at the time was that I was **afraid of stepping into my highest potential.** Not because I didn't want it—but because it was so unfamiliar. Growth felt uncertain. Who would I be without my old roles? What if I failed? What if I succeeded? What if people didn't like this new version of me?

Then I realised: *I was waiting for permission to expand. But no one was coming to give it to me. I had to choose it myself.*

The shift didn't happen overnight. It happened in small, intentional moments where I stopped waiting and started embodying.

Practical Exercise: Embodying Your Future Self

Your future self already exists. The work now is to bring them into your present reality.

Step 1: Meeting Your Future Self

Journal Prompt: *"Who is the version of me that has already healed, expanded, and stepped into their highest potential? What do they think, feel, and believe?"*

Try This: Close your eyes and **visualise your future self** standing in front of you. Notice their energy, their posture, their ease. Imagine stepping into their body. Feel what they feel. Let that feeling settle into your present self.

Step 2: Embodying the Future Self in the Present

Somatic Practice:

- Choose **one action per day** that aligns with your future self. This could be how you speak, how you set boundaries, how you carry yourself, or how you start your morning.
- Every time you feel resistance, remind yourself: *"I am already becoming this version of me."*

Step 3: Releasing Attachments to Old Identities

Affirmation Practice:

- "I release the need to shrink to stay in alignment with my past."
- "I allow myself to expand into the fullest expression of who I am."
- "I trust myself to step into my future with confidence."

You Are Already Becoming

You are not waiting for healing to be complete before stepping into your power.

You are not waiting for external validation before choosing to trust yourself.

You are not waiting for permission before expanding into your full potential.

You are already becoming. You are already shifting. You are already stepping into the life that was always meant for you.

The only thing left to do is keep walking forward.

Chapter 13: Integrating the Journey & Moving Forward

"The journey isn't about becoming someone new. It's about remembering who you were before the world told you who to be." – Unknown

The End of This Chapter, The Beginning of a New One

You have done the deep work. You have uncovered your masks, rewritten your stories, reclaimed your power, and stepped into your authenticity. But this is not the end—it is the **beginning of a lifelong practice of self-trust, expansion, and living in alignment.**

Healing does not have a finish line. Growth does not have an expiration date. The work you have done in this book is **not about perfection—it is about integration.** The real magic happens in the moments when you choose yourself, over and over again.

This final chapter will explore:

- How to continue integrating everything you've learned.
- How to navigate the inevitable changes that come with authenticity.
- The importance of ongoing self-inquiry and embodiment.
- A final guided practice for stepping fully into your authentic life.

By the end of this chapter, you will have a **clear roadmap for continuing forward**—not just with knowledge, but with embodied wisdom.

Integration: Turning Awareness Into Embodiment

Awareness is the first step. But embodiment is where the transformation truly happens.

Many people complete their healing journey only to feel **lost once the intensity of self-discovery settles.** It's normal to ask, *"What now?"* The answer is simple:

- Keep practicing.
- Keep showing up.
- Keep choosing yourself, even when it feels uncomfortable.

The work does not end when the book is closed. **Integration means taking what you've learned and making it part of your daily life.**

Part of that integration is recognising when you are stepping into resistance.

Resistance is the **internal pushback** we experience when facing change, growth, or deep emotional work. It often **disguises itself as procrastination, doubt, distraction, or even a sudden urge to quit altogether.**

Resistance is not a sign that something is wrong—it's **a natural response from the nervous system**, trying to keep us **safe within familiar patterns.** It shows up when we're about to break through old conditioning, challenge long-held beliefs, or step into something unknown.

You may **recognise resistance** as:

- **Feeling stuck, overwhelmed, or exhausted** whenever you try to do the inner work.
- **Self-sabotaging** by avoiding, numbing, or convincing yourself it's "not the right time."
- **Becoming hyper-critical** of yourself or the process, dismissing your progress.
- **A sudden urge to abandon healing altogether** and return to old habits, even if they no longer serve you.

The key to working through resistance is **awareness.** Instead of fighting it, **acknowledge it as part of the process.** Resistance does not mean you are failing—it means you are on the edge of transformation.

The more we meet resistance with curiosity rather than avoidance, the more we can **move through it instead of being controlled by it.**

The Realities of Growth: Navigating Change & Resistance

As you step into this new version of yourself, you will encounter challenges:

- Some people may not understand or support your growth, and that is okay.
- Old patterns may try to pull you back into familiar roles.
- Your nervous system may resist expansion because it is unfamiliar.

This is not a sign to stop. It is a sign that you are growing beyond what you once knew.

- Trust that the relationships meant for you will adjust to the real you.
- Trust that the discomfort of change is temporary, but the freedom of authenticity is lasting.
- Trust that you are capable of navigating what comes next.

Belinda's Personal Story: Living Authentically in the Real World

"

I thought the hardest part of healing was doing the inner work. I was wrong. The hardest part was living that work in a world that still expected me to be my old self."

Once I had done the deep healing, I expected everything to feel different. And in many ways, it did. But I wasn't prepared for the moments when **old patterns, familiar dynamics, and external expectations tried to pull me back.**

I had to learn that integration meant choosing myself **not just in solitude, but in relationships, in work, and in every area of life.**

I had to remind myself: *Just because it's uncomfortable doesn't mean it's wrong. Growth is uncomfortable. Expansion is unfamiliar. And that's okay.*

Now, every time I feel doubt, fear, or resistance, I remind myself: *I didn't come this far just to stop. I came this far to live fully.*

And you have too.

Practical Exercise: Creating Your Personal Integration Plan

Step 1: Identify Your Core Commitments to Yourself

Journal Prompt: *"What are three things I commit to doing daily, weekly, and monthly to stay connected to my authentic self?"*

Try This: Make a **non-negotiable list** of actions that keep you aligned (e.g., setting boundaries, self-care, movement, creative expression).

Step 2: Build a Support System

Reflection Exercise:

- Identify three people or spaces where you feel truly safe and seen.
- If you don't have them yet, commit to seeking aligned relationships that support your growth.

Step 3: Honour the Journey & Celebrate the Work

Affirmation Practice:

> *"I am proud of the work I have done. I trust myself to continue."*

> *"I do not have to be perfect. I only have to keep choosing myself."*

> *"I am safe to expand, to feel, to thrive."*

You Are Free to Be Fully Yourself

The version of you that was conditioned to hide, shrink, or suppress is no longer in control.

You have stepped into something greater.

You have reclaimed your voice, your truth, your power.

You have come home to yourself. You are allowed to take up space - as much as you like!

And now, the only thing left to do is to live.

<u>Fully. Authentically. Unapologetically.</u>

This is your beginning.

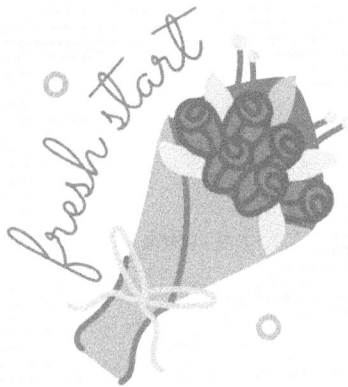

Final Word from Belinda

If you've made it to this page, I want you to pause for a moment and take a deep breath.

You did this. You chose yourself. Well done!

You sat with truths that were once hidden. You faced patterns that were generations in the making. You acknowledged pain that was never yours to carry. And through it all, you kept going.

I know what it feels like to question if you're doing it "right." To wonder if you've changed enough. To feel the weight of old stories trying to pull you back. But here's what I want you to remember: **You are not back where you started. Every time you choose yourself, you are breaking cycles that were never meant to be yours. Every time you choose your truth over fear; you are rewriting the future.**

There is no "end" to this journey. The work of being real, of being fully yourself, is a daily practice. And some days, you will forget. Some days, you will slip into old patterns. Some days, it will feel easier to go back to what is familiar. That's okay.

You do not have to be perfect to be worthy of the life you desire. You only have to be willing.

So, as you close this book and step forward, I want to leave you with this: **You are not alone. You are seen. You are capable. And no matter what happens next, you are always allowed to choose yourself again.**

With gratitude and belief in you,
Belinda

About the Author

Belinda Evans is a **Holistic Wellness Practitioner and Somatic & Integrative Healing Specialist**, blending trauma-informed therapy, nervous system healing, and holistic beauty therapy and metaphysics into a unique, whole-person approach. With over **15+ years of experience**, she specialises in helping individuals break free from conditioning, releasing stored trauma, and step into their authentic selves in whichever way is aligned for them.

As the driving force behind **Emjay Spa & Wellness** (www.emjayspa.com), Belinda has expanded its offerings beyond traditional beauty therapy, creating a space where **inner healing meets outer transformation**. Through her work, she bridges the gap between **mind, body, and soul**, offering a compassionate, intuitive, and deeply personal approach to wellness.

When she's not working with clients, Belinda is passionate about **personal growth, holistic healing, and self-discovery**. Her work is dedicated to guiding people toward **self-trust, emotional freedom, and a more empowered way of living**.

Continue Your Journey

Your healing, transformation and self-discovery journey doesn't end with this book—it continues with how you choose to integrate this work into your life.

If you'd like to deepen your journey, you can:

- Join Emjay's private Facebook groups, membership programs and explore the range of courses available as all are spaces for ongoing support, insights, and connection.
- Explore additional steps. resources, workshops, and coaching at www.emjayspa.com

Leave a review! Your feedback helps others find this book and start their own transformation.

You are not alone in this. Keep going. Keep choosing yourself. And know that you are always enough.

www.ingramcontent.com/pod-product-compliance
Lightning Source LLC
Chambersburg PA
CBHW072355090426
42741CB00012B/3039